Look Alive

Look Alive

BEHIND THE SCENES OF AN ANIMATED FILM

WRITTEN BY
Elaine Scott

PHOTOGRAPHS BY
Richard Hewett

MORROW JUNIOR BOOKS • New York

ACKNOWLEDGMENTS

We would like to thank George McQuilkin, John and Niki Matthews, Tom Smith, Joel Fletcher, Ray Greer, Michael Belzer, and Fred Schaefer for patiently answering questions, drawing diagrams, and sharing their enthusiasm for this project with us. Additional thanks go to John Matthews and Joel Fletcher for producing the images of Ralph on the corner of the pages.

And, of course, we thank Beverly Cleary, whose books began it all.

Videocassettes of *Ralph S. Mouse* are available for schools and libraries from Churchill Films, Inc., 12210 Nebraska Avenue, Los Angeles, California 90025.

Book design by Trish Parcell Watts.

Library of Congress Cataloging-in-Publication Data
Scott, Elaine, 1940-
Look alive : behind the scenes of an animated film / written by Elaine Scott ; photographs by Richard Hewett.
p.   cm.
Includes index.
Summary: Provides an insider's view of the making of the animated movie "Ralph S. Mouse," in which stop-action animation and other special effects are used to bring a puppet to life as the character from three popular Beverly Cleary books.
ISBN 0-688-09936-X. — ISBN 0-688-09937-8 (library)
1. Ralph S. Mouse (Motion picture)—Juvenile literature.
[1. Ralph S. Mouse (Motion picture) 2. Puppet films. 3. Motion pictures—Production and direction.] I. Hewett, Richard, ill.
II. Title.
PN1997.R2343   1992
791.43'72—dc20   91-36220   CIP   AC

PHOTO AND ART CREDITS
Permission for photographs is gratefully acknowledged: The Bettmann Archive, p. 5; © Buena Vista Pictures Distribution, Inc., p. 4; California Raisin Advisory Board, p. 56; © 1991 King Features Syndicate, p. 12; Margaret Miller, p. 2; The Museum of Modern Art/Film Stills Archive, pp. 4, 6; The Walt Disney Company, pp. 58, 60.
The artwork on pages 13 and 18 is by John Matthews. The corner-page images of the mouse used throughout the book were created by Joel Fletcher and John Matthews.

FOR MY BROTHER, GEORGE,
WHO STILL LOVES CARTOONS
WITH MY LOVE

—E. S.

Contents

Look Alive

Introduction

Ralph S. Mouse is one of the best-known rodents in children's literature. Readers all over the world have followed his adventures in Beverly Cleary's novels *The Mouse and the Motorcycle, Runaway Ralph,* and *Ralph S. Mouse.* In the stories, Ralph is a friendly and curious mouse who talks but is understood only by Matt, the handyman at the Mountain View Inn, and lonely children who share Ralph's interest in "fast cars and motorcycles and who took the trouble to listen," as the author has explained.

The stories about Ralph and his adventures had their beginnings in a true incident. When the Clearys' son, Malcolm, was a young boy, he became ill while the family was vacationing. Beverly Cleary remembers that she bought her son a toy motorcycle to play with and that, for a while, there was no aspirin to bring his fever down. Much later, after the family had returned home, a neighbor called her over to see a mouse that had tumbled into a watering can.

"I remember thinking at the time that the mouse was just the size to fit Malcolm's motorcycle," Beverly Cleary said as she smiled at the memory. A mouse, just the right size for a toy motorcycle, and a boy who needed an aspirin—from these two incidents, the idea for the first of three novels about the adventures of a boylike mouse was born. *The Mouse and the Motorcycle* tells the story of a young boy who needed an aspirin when all the stores in town were closed and Ralph, the sympathetic motorcycle-riding mouse who finally—after many trials—delivers it. When the book was published, it delighted readers around the world, as did the two sequels, *Runaway Ralph* and *Ralph S. Mouse*.

With the exception of her autobiography, *A Girl from Yamhill*, the stories Beverly Cleary writes are fiction, which means she creates them from her imagination. Some stories, such as the ones she has written about Ramona Quimby, are realistic fiction. What happens to the Quimbys could happen to any family. However, the stories about Ralph are a kind of fiction called *fantasy*. What happens to Ralph, Matt, and the boys who come to stay at the Mountain View Inn could never happen in real life. In reality, boys can get sick while they are on vacation, and they may need an aspirin, but mice cannot talk—and they can't ride motorcycles or drive ambulances, either.

Beverly Cleary is the author of over forty well-loved books for young readers.

Nevertheless, in a good fantasy novel, the author must be able to write in such a way that readers believe the story really happened—at least while they are reading it.

It isn't easy to write good fantasy, and George Mc-Quilkin is one person who knows that. Part of George's job as president of Churchill Entertainment, a division of Churchill Films, requires him to read hundreds of children's books in order to find ones that Churchill could use as the basis for television specials and videos for schools and libraries.

As president of Churchill Entertainment, George McQuilkin is in charge of all films the company produces.

When George finished reading the books about Ralph S. Mouse, he knew that he wanted to make films of them. "I love those stories," he says. "They are a wonderful combination of reality and fantasy."

Just as making a reader believe that a mouse can talk is an equal challenge for an experienced author such as Beverly Cleary, bringing that mouse to life on the screen is a challenge even for an experienced animator. George McQuilkin said, "Five-year-olds watching our Ralph movies ask, 'How'd you get a mouse to do that?' They absolutely believe what they are seeing. Nine-year-old boys and girls are a bit more sophisticated, however. They are willing to believe while they watch the show, but afterward they ask, 'How'd *you* do that?' "

"How'd you do that?" is a question film audiences have asked ever since a gorilla named King Kong appeared to straddle the Empire State Building, clutching a young woman in one hand while he swatted planes from the sky with his other. *King Kong* was one of the first films to use animation. It made its debut in movie theaters over fifty years ago, and led the way for hundreds of animated films and films that used some animation, such as *Snow White and the Seven Dwarfs; Cinderella; Jaws; Star Wars; Honey, I Shrunk the Kids;* and, more recently, *Who Framed Roger Rabbit?* These films feature different kinds of animation, and each animator hopes that the audience will watch his or her film and wonder, How'd they do that? Perhaps you, too, have wondered how this magic is created.

People have been trying to show figures in motion ever

3

King Kong created a sensation when he appeared on movie screens in 1933.

Three-dimensional animation creates a terrifying ant. (*Honey, I Shrunk the Kids* © Buena Vista Pictures Distribution, Inc.)

since prehistoric artists living in Altamira, Spain, drew horses with six or more legs on the walls of their caves. However, no one looking at those early attempts to show motion would believe those animals were actually moving. The art just wasn't realistic.

Thousands of centuries later, the invention of photography resulted in very realistic images for people to view; however, there was still no motion in them. People and animals were frozen forever in their photographic poses. Unlike today's snapshots, the early photographs were produced on pieces of glass. Each new picture required a fresh piece of glass in the camera. Then, in 1887, a man named Hannibal Goodwin took a piece of transparent material called *celluloid* and coated it with a special chemical film that was sensitive to light. When the celluloid was exposed to light, an image was retained on it. About the same time, George Eastman was in the business of manufacturing photographic equipment. He saw that Goodwin's new coated celluloid had many advantages over the old glass plates, which broke and took only one picture per piece of glass. Eastman began to manufacture the celluloid under the name of Eastman film.

The American inventor Thomas Edison decided to work with this new Eastman film to see whether he could make pictures that actually appeared to move. Edison invented a box, which he called a *kinetoscope*. A person looked at the film through a peephole in the box, winding it off one spool and onto another by a hand crank. The pictures inside the box appeared to move. Next, Edison invented a projecting kinetoscope. The film was projected onto a screen and many people could watch at once. On April 23, 1896, Thomas Edison revealed his new invention at the Koster and Bial's Music Hall in New York City. His projected film showed a prizefight, a dancer, and waves rolling onto the beach. The movies had been born.

In the beginning, moving pictures were a novelty. People watched them in the same way they looked at any other curiosity; they were interesting for a while, but soon the audience became bored. Something was missing from the movies—a story. In 1903, an American film director,

Moving pictures first appeared in a kinetoscope.

Edwin S. Porter, realized that audiences wanted something other than a series of scenes to watch, and so he made a film about men who robbed a train, were chased, and were finally captured. *The Great Train Robbery* lasted eleven minutes and was a huge success. People across the country flocked to theaters called nickelodeons (because it cost a nickel for admission), and the movies were on their way to becoming an institution in American life.

Improvements were made all the time. The stories became longer and more complicated. In the late 1920s, sound was introduced. Now, the characters could talk. By

The Great Train Robbery was a box office smash in 1903.

the 1930s, filmmakers were experimenting with animation, and the first nonhuman film actors such as King Kong and Mickey Mouse were created. Audiences around the world came to love animated films and looked forward eagerly to the cartoons that preceded each feature film. Cartoon characters became as real to film audiences as their human counterparts.

By the 1950s, television sets were beginning to appear in most American homes, and animated features became a staple of children's broadcasting, as they are today. Through the years animation has improved, just as filmmaking has improved. Today, it is one of the most sophisticated forms of the art and an important part of the film industry.

The dictionary says *to animate* means "to bring something to life." Although Ralph always has seemed alive to those who read about him in Beverly Cleary's novels, this book will let you read about how Churchill Entertainment and its chief animator, John Matthews, brought him to life for the thousands who watch his adventures on television screens around the world.

Ralph waits on the set, ready to go to work.

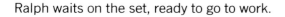

CHAPTER ONE

Getting Permission

The process of creating movies or television specials is divided into three segments: preproduction, production, and postproduction. Production is the time when the actors are actually being filmed. Anything that occurs before that time is called preproduction, and any activity that takes place after that time is called postproduction.

Many decisions must be made during the preproduction process, and one of the first for an animated film is choosing the right animator for the project. In talking about the Ralph movies, George McQuilkin said, "I loved the challenge of combining an animated mouse with real people in a film, and I knew it would be just the right challenge for animator John Matthews."

George McQuilkin and John Matthews have worked together for years on many different Churchill projects. John had read the Ralph books to his sons, and he was eager to create the perfect mouse for the films.

After John and George had discussed the Ralph project, they were ready to take the next step in the preproduction process—acquiring the necessary rights, or permissions to make the films. Beverly Cleary and her publisher, William Morrow and Company, Inc., owned all of the rights to the stories about Ralph, so George McQuilkin arranged a meeting with Mrs. Cleary to explain his plans for the film to her.

"I told her how much John and I loved the stories about Ralph, and how eager we were to make television specials of them," George said, remembering that first visit.

Mrs. Cleary knew that, in addition to many other projects, George and John had worked together to produce films of Arnold Lobel's classic stories about Frog and Toad. Those films were carefully made and won many prestigious awards, and she felt that George and John would exercise the same kind of care if they made films of her books.

Next came a discussion of which rights Churchill wanted to purchase. When some books are adapted for movies or television shows, the producers purchase the rights to the author's characters, as well as to the stories themselves. If that happens, the resulting show does not necessarily have to be true to the story in the book. For example, the television series *Little House on the Prairie* was based on the characters in Laura Ingalls Wilder's

books. Although the characters were the same, the stories that appeared on television were written by scriptwriters and were not the same as the ones created by Mrs. Wilder.

Beverly Cleary has never sold the rights to her characters. However, she has sold the film rights to portions of some of her stories about Ramona Quimby and the three novels about Ralph. Mrs. Cleary did not write the scripts for any of the shows about Ramona or Ralph that have appeared on television. Instead, scriptwriters have done that work.

When authors write novels, they usually talk about what is going on inside their characters' heads—what they are thinking or feeling. Readers know that Ralph is sad, or angry, or frightened and lonely when they read sentences such as, "Ralph experienced the darkest moment of his life"; or "Ralph thought of the old hotel with its shabby lobby warmed by a crackling fire. He missed the reassuring tick of the rasping old clock"; or "Of course, Ralph's feelings were hurt."

Scriptwriters, on the other hand, must tell their story not so much with words as with pictures. In many television shows and movies, there will be long scenes without dialogue—no talking—but the camera will still tell a story. A shot of Ralph pacing on a windowsill or merrily riding across the lobby floor on his motorcycle or Laser XL7 tells the audience a lot about how he is feeling without any words being said. It is important, however, when dialogue is spoken that it stays as true to the character as possible. Ralph must always sound like Beverly

When everyone has gone to bed, Ralph rides his motorcycle through the Mountain View Inn.

Cleary's Ralph, so choosing the right people to write the scripts was an important part of the discussion during the meeting between Beverly Cleary and George McQuilkin. Joe S. Landon was chosen to be the scriptwriter for *Ralph S. Mouse*. Mrs. Cleary requested script consultation rights, which means that as the scripts were written, she read them and made suggestions for changes she thought were needed.

The Mouse and the Motorcycle was the first book about Ralph that Beverly Cleary wrote. It was also the first film about him that Churchill Entertainment made. During the discussion of rights for this film, the question of animation came up. One choice they had was cellular animation, which is two-dimensional, or flat. The common name for this kind of animation is cartoon, and cartoons have been popular for fifty years. Mickey Mouse, Donald Duck, Woody Woodpecker, Popeye, and the Flintstones are just a few examples of famous cartoon characters that have come to life through the magic of cellular animation.

On the other hand, they had the option of using three-dimensional animation, which uses puppets and other three-dimensional figures to achieve its effects. As the name implies, three-dimensional animated figures are not flat; they have height, width, and depth. R2D2 from *Star Wars*, E.T. from the film of the same name, and the ants and bees in *Honey, I Shrunk the Kids* are all examples of three-dimensional animated figures.

Beverly Cleary did not want a cartoon mouse, and nei-

Popeye is a popular celluloid sailor. (© King Features Syndicate.)

ther did George McQuilkin. During the initial visit, there was some discussion of using live mice, but as George said, "Real mice are difficult to control, and anyway, real mice can't act sad, or be contrite, or show all the emotions that Ralph shows in the books."

Then Mrs. Cleary suggested using finger puppets, and she brought out a mouse finger puppet that she happened to have.

George smiled when he saw the puppet and said, "That's similar to what we had in mind, only John's puppet is more elaborate." With that comment, George produced a

drawing that John Matthews had done. It was of a mouse, sitting on its hind legs. A cutaway version showed an elaborate system of ball-and-socket joints that allowed the mouse to move, blink its eyes, and grasp things with its paws. Cables ran from the mouse to a box with levers that controlled them. All in all, the mouse looked like something created in a mad scientist's laboratory.

When she saw the drawing, Beverly Cleary promptly dubbed it "the B–52 Mouse." It was clear that John had thought a lot about Ralph and it was obvious that when he was built, he would be a special mouse indeed.

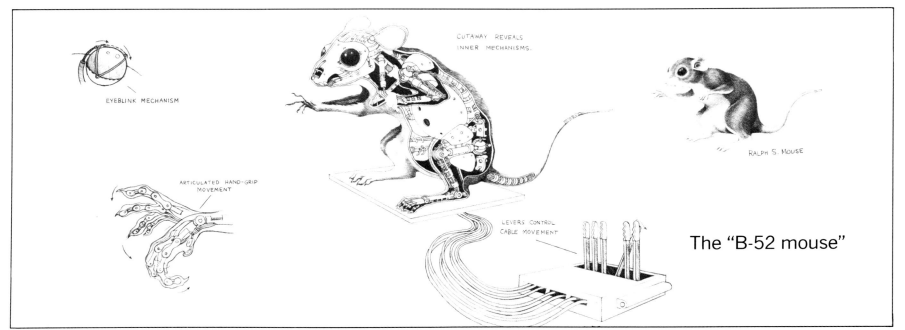

EYEBLINK MECHANISM

ARTICULATED HAND-GRIP MOVEMENT

CUTAWAY REVEALS INNER MECHANISMS.

RALPH S. MOUSE

LEVERS CONTROL CABLE MOVEMENT

The "B-52 mouse"

·

CHAPTER TWO

Getting Ready

Once Churchill had acquired the rights to *Ralph S. Mouse*, the next step in the preproduction process began: finding the money to make the film.

Television specials cost a great deal of money to produce. George McQuilkin said, "The only way a rather small company like Churchill Entertainment can afford to do a show like this is with financial backing from a large television network. We were delighted when ABC expressed an interest in the project."

As they had with *The Mouse and the Motorcycle* and *Runaway Ralph*, the people in charge of children's programming at ABC wanted to license *Ralph S. Mouse* and make the film a part of the network's Saturday-morning series called ABC Weekend Specials. Since Churchill Entertainment owned the television rights to the Ralph stories, ABC paid

The star of the show, Ralph S. Mouse

licensing-fee money to finance the production of *Ralph S. Mouse*. And like the other two stories about Ralph, this one was shown as a two-part special, with each segment lasting a half hour. Although each part of the Ralph specials takes up thirty minutes of airtime, each segment of the story is told in only twenty-two minutes. The other eight minutes are used for commercials, station breaks, and public-service announcements.

Once the money was in hand, George McQuilkin and John Matthews carefully planned how it would be spent. All films and television shows have budgets. If the show is completely animated, such as *All Dogs Go to Heaven*, there will be one budget. If, however, the film will use a combination of animation and live action, such as *Who Framed Roger Rabbit?* or *E.T.*, there may be two budgets. *Ralph S. Mouse* had two budgets: One was set up for the live-action part of the film, in which human actors such as Robert Oliveri, Ray Walston, and Karen Black appear as Ryan, Matt, and Miss Kuckenbacker. The other budget was for the animation, which stars a puppet named Ralph. In addition to the budgets, each segment of the filming had its own time schedule. The live action took only two weeks to film. The animation took months to complete.

However, before either segment could begin, the sets had to be built and furnished. John Matthews designed all of the sets for *Ralph S. Mouse*. As he said, "I had to do the designing, because of the constraints of animation. I knew where holes had to be drilled in the walls and furniture, in order to run the cables that control Ralph."

Churchill a sum of money—called a licensing fee—in exchange for the right to show each of the Ralph films as many times as ABC wants for ten years.

As in the other two films, George McQuilkin used the

First, John made detailed sketches of how he wanted the rooms and the furniture to look. Using the sketches as a guide, John and his team constructed the sets over a month-long period. At the end of that time, the lobby of the Mountain View Inn, Ryan's bedroom, his class at school, and Mr. Costa's workroom all had come to life inside Churchill's Los Angeles studio.

Working in his studio at home, John Matthews sketches the sets for the film.

John wanted the Mountain View Inn to have different furniture from what it had in the other two shows. Since Mrs. Cleary's stories are fantasies, John decided that a forest motif, with lots of bears, would be fun, even though he realized that this was not the lobby described in the book. In *Ralph S. Mouse* the grandfather clock that provides shelter for Ralph's nest looks like an old tree, and a bear peeks out from a large knothole in its hollow trunk. Later, John animated the bear so he would turn his head from side to side in imitation of a pendulum.

In order to create this fanciful furniture, John and his assistants went to work, carving branches and bears out of artist's foam. The foam is easy to work with; however, when it is cut, it gives off dangerous particles that, if inhaled, could cause a serious lung disease. Therefore, all John's sculptors wore masks while they worked, to filter the particles of foam out of the air they breathed. When they were finished, the Mountain View Inn looked old and tired, as Beverly Cleary had described it—and also a bit mysterious. It seemed like just the place where a mouse could talk to a handyman and a lonely young boy.

During this time, model maker Ray Greer built the maze that Ralph must run through, following closely the illustration in the book. However, other special devices that were not in the book appear in the film. They were designed and constructed just for the television show in order to use more animation. Ray Greer took a large floor buffer—a machine that polishes floors—and gave it headlights and a revolving light. The floor buffer became an

Opposite page: John's completed sketch for the lobby of the Mountain View Inn

This page: Following John's design, the carpenters create the sets in the studio.

Ray Greer puts the finishing touches on Mr. Costa's self-propelled floor buffer.

important prop when it took off on its own, chasing Mr. Costa and wrapping him up in its cord. John also designed a special mousetrap for Mr. Costa to use in his pursuit of Ralph. The trap came complete with the alluring smell of cheese and twinkling lights to entice Ralph to walk up its treadmill entrance. Even John's young sons, Nathan; Nigel, Ryan, and Sam, got into the act by planting seeds

in Styrofoam cups and making bean mosaics to hang on the classroom's walls.

One special prop needed to be built for this show—the Laser XL7 car. In the book Ralph's motorcycle was broken during a fight between Ryan and Brad. Brad eventually gives Ralph his beloved XL7 sports car to make up for it.

Joel Fletcher creates a windshield for the Laser XL7.

20

Obviously, Ralph was going to need a Laser XL7 for the television special, so John asked his animator, Joel Fletcher, to make one.

Joel went to work, using parts from several complicated model kits. In one kit, the car came with a bubble top, but Joel had to turn that into a windshield when he discovered that Ralph's ears were too large to fit under the dome. Joel worked on that special car for days. When he was finished, the Laser XL7 had working headlights, taillights, turn indicators, plus real steering and suspension mechanisms.

Joel has worked for John for several years now, and he still loves his job. As he said, "When I was a kid, I always liked to draw, sculpt, and make models. I still love to do it, but now I get paid for it. Animation is a serious business, but if you want to do it well, you have to keep a certain childlike quality." Joel loved making the Laser XL7 so much that he asked to be allowed to keep the car when the filming was complete—as part of his salary! It is a sports car to delight a man, or a boy . . . or a mouse.

Budgets and sets are important parts of the preproduction period for any television show or movie. The most important part of preproduction for this particular show, however, was the creation of its star—Ralph S. Mouse. Without a believable mouse, there would be no television special.

CHAPTER THREE

·

Making Mice

As anyone who has read the books about him knows, Ralph is no ordinary mouse. He rides motorcycles, wears crash helmets, and worries about his family and friends. As John Matthews said, "Ralph has a soul, a real personality." For John, then, the trick was to design a mouse with a personality and a soul, who nevertheless still behaves and looks like a mouse and not a cartoon character.

John has been designing things for years—ever since he was in high school. In fact, during his senior year in high school, he entered an architectural competition in which the contestants were to design a complete house. Entries came from all over the Los Angeles area. A construction company announced that they actually would build the house that had the winning design. John won that contest. Recently, he said proudly, "Somewhere in Pasadena, California, someone is living in a house that I designed in high school."

After such an accomplishment, a career in architecture seemed a natural next step for the high school boy, and he enrolled in college, determined to study that field. "I got so bored, I fell asleep over the drafting table," John said. "It just didn't interest me."

What did interest John were his art history and art appreciation classes, and writing music. Later, he took classes in animation and making puppets. "And," he added, "I went out and bought a book called *Animation in Ten Hard Lessons* and studied every page of it."

When John met his wife, Niki, she was interested in making puppets. The two of them worked together to create them, then used their creations to do shows and workshops for schools and libraries. About this time, Churchill Films was looking for someone to make large puppets for a film they wanted to make on nutrition. The company hired John to create a villain for the film. John created a puppet representing a blob of fat and named it Blubber McGreasy. His career in animation was on its way!

John and Niki worked on several other Churchill projects, including the Frog and Toad stories by Arnold Lobel. John began his work on the Ralph projects by studying real mice, watching the way they moved. Different species of animals move in different ways. John explained that mice have different nervous systems from cats, for ex-

John and Niki Matthews have worked together for years.

24

ample. "Mice are more nervous, and their movements are a lot jumpier," he said.

Next, he made sketches of all the mice in Mrs. Cleary's novels. Each mouse had his own look and his own personality, and John gave each of them a name, even if they have no name in the story. "I always name all of my puppets," he said. "I'm superstitious about that." Toots, Wilbur, and Sly are some of the names John has given to Mrs. Cleary's rough outdoor mice.

When the sketches are complete, it is time to bring the puppet to life. If the characters are drawn, as they are in the two-dimensional cel animation, their movement is controlled by the number of cels, or pictures, the artist creates. However, the kind of three-dimensional animation John was doing with Ralph required a puppet, and the first step in the puppet-making process is creating a skeleton, or armature, as it is properly called. After that, the armature must assume a shape—mouse, human, monster—whatever the animator needs for his show. Shapes are created by making molds, then foam-rubber flesh is added to the mold, and when the foam rubber dries, or sets, details are put on the puppet. It is a delicate and time-consuming job that requires patience, artistic skill, and a bit of mechanical engineering!

The puppet's movement is controlled by its armature, and animators say that a puppet is only as good as the armature it has. John designs all the armatures for his puppets himself, then he and his team of animators care-

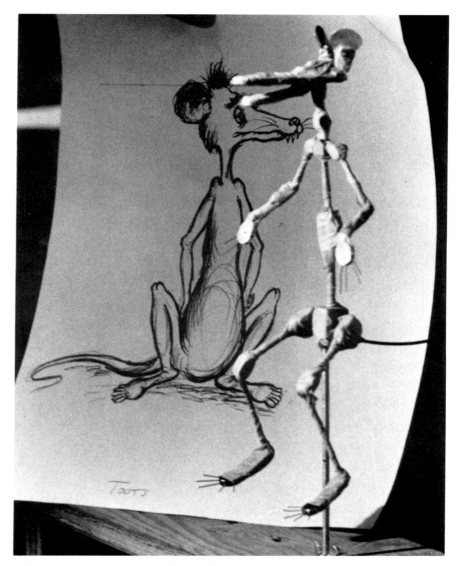

John sketched a mouse, then built the armature.

25

fully build them. They use thousands of pieces of solid brass and steel to construct ball-and-socket joints, wire hinges, and tiny "bones." When the skeletons are completed, they are tested to be certain that each joint moves smoothly and easily, with just the right amount of pressure. The secret of all good animation lies in the way the figure moves; to be believable, the movements must be smooth, not jerky. If a joint is too loose or too tight, the animator will not be able to adjust the position of the puppet as precisely as he wants—perhaps a mere fraction of an inch—when it is time to do the animation.

Brass and the ingredients that make the foam-rubber flesh do not react well together, so, next, the armatures are wrapped in strips of latex or heavy-duty tape to protect them from the foam while they are baking in the mold. Making that mold is the next step in the process.

In creating the mice for *Ralph S. Mouse*, clay was carefully pressed over the wrapped skeleton, then it was sculpted to look like the mouse in John's sketch. After the last detail of the sculpture was completed, a coat of shellac was applied. When it dried, the model got a very thin coat of petroleum jelly to help ease it out of the mold after it was set.

The sculpted mouse was placed in a box and clay was pressed around its bottom half, around every curve of its body, between each finger and toe, then was carefully spread to the sides of the box. Five indentations, or keyholes, were put into the clay around the figure. When the

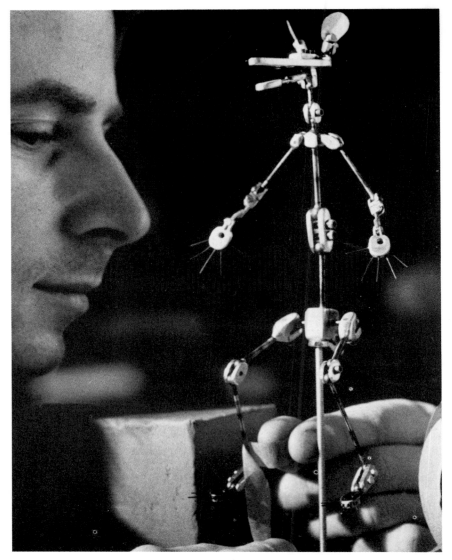

The brass armature must be covered with tape or strips of latex.

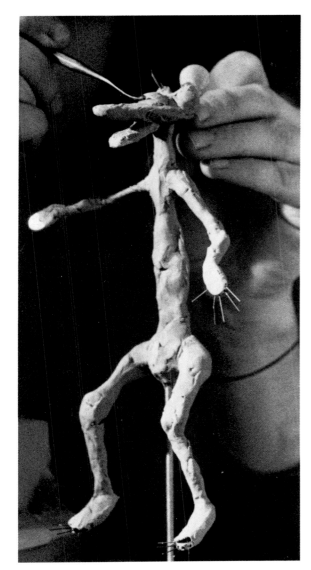

Clay is pressed over the wrapped armature.

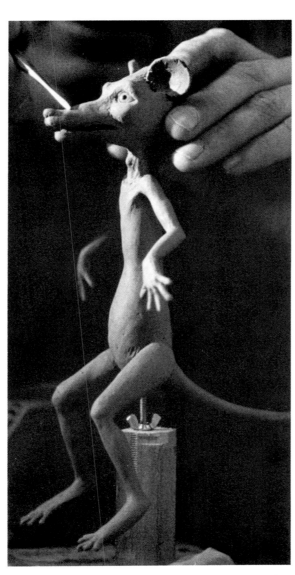

The clay is sculpted to look like John's sketch.

A coat of shellac gives a finishing touch.

mold was cast, these holes were fitted with four matching bumps from the other side, which helped to hold the two halves of the mold together.

"This part of the process is a real art," John said. "The seams of the mold are very important. Both sides must fit together perfectly. The mold can't shift during the foam process."

Since the molds were used more than once, John chose a special kind of resin plaster to make them. Resin plasters must be mixed with a chemical agent, or catalyst, to make them work, but they are very durable when they harden. John said, "I use Ultracal. It's a dental plaster, and it's *hard*. I can get about three puppets from an Ultracal mold." After three puppets were cast, some of the details in the mold began to wear away.

Once mixed, the plaster was poured very carefully to avoid bubbles getting into it. The plaster had to cover the mouse in the mold completely, and bubbles could have created pockets of air around the model. "Bubbles can ruin you," John explained.

When the plaster hardened, the sides of the mold were removed. Some of the plaster might have seeped underneath the model, so the back of the mouse was cleaned to expose all of the details of its sculpting. Once again, the process of mixing and pouring the plaster was repeated. When this half was completed, the clay model was removed from the mold. The carefully sculpted mouse was broken and the armature was saved. It was used later in the process when it was inserted inside its foam flesh.

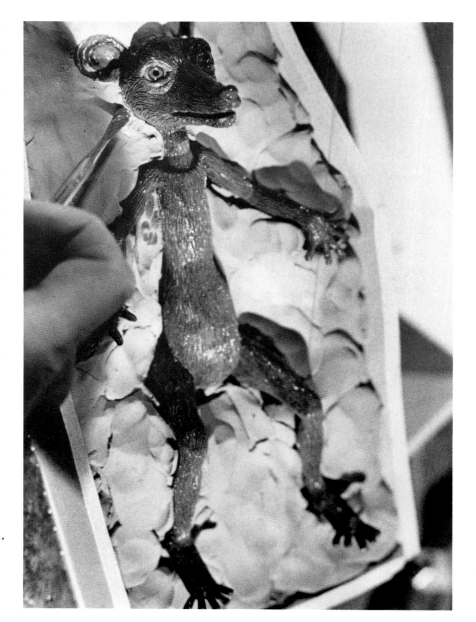

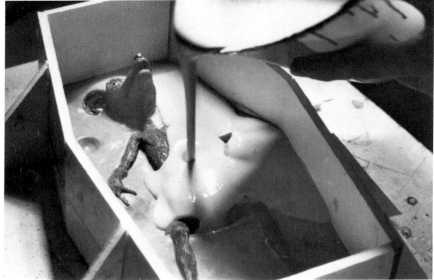

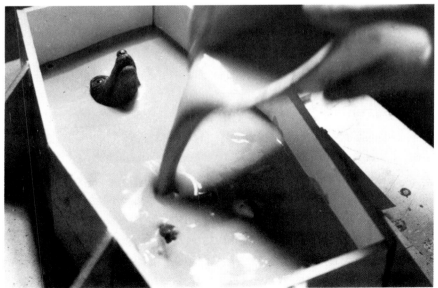

Opposite page: More clay is pressed around the mouse, between each finger and toe.

This page, above left: The clay is smoothed out, and keyholes are placed around the sides of the mold.

Above right: Then the plaster is carefully poured...

Below right: until the mouse completely disappears beneath it.

With the model removed, the mold is ready for the foam rubber mixture.

very porous, with lots of large bubbles in it. However, the kind Niki made for the puppet's skin was finely textured, with almost invisible bubbles. Niki measured the foam ingredients into a bowl and used her mixer to beat them together, just as if she had been making a cake. The armature was placed back into the mold, then Niki poured her foam mixture over it, slipped it into her oven, and baked it at 250 degrees for about four hours. Unlike baking a cake, the baking puppet did not fill the Matthews's kitchen with a delicious smell. "It really stinks the house up," Niki said, and Sam added, "It smells just like rotten eggs."

When the baking is complete, Niki carefully opens the mold.

With the mold and armature removed, all that was left were two molds that had concave impressions of the front and back of the mouse. Now it was time for Niki to work her magic. Out of this hollow, empty space, she would pull forth mice—made out of foam rubber.

Niki worked at home, mixing the foam for the mice in her kitchen. Foam rubber comes in many different consistencies. Some, like the kind used for many sponges, is

When the puppet was "cooked," Niki gently removed it from the mold, working as carefully as she could to avoid tearing the delicate foam. She used manicure scissors to trim away the flashing, or excess foam that surrounded the puppet's body and clung between its fingers and toes. When that task was finished, she was ready to give the mouse some fur.

The foam tears easily, so removing the puppet from the mold is always a tense moment.

Ralph gets a coat of fur.

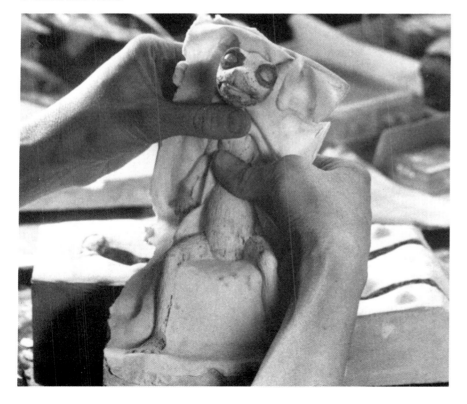

Niki used the fur of winter weasels, or ermines, because, as she explained, "It's much more resilient than other kinds of fur. The puppets are handled a lot and this fur will spring back if it's been crushed." Winter weasels are white, however, and the mice in Mrs. Cleary's stories are brown field mice, so Niki had to dye the ermine skins a mouselike brown before she could begin the furring process.

Next, she painted the puppet, giving Ralph's ears, paws, tail, and nose a mouselike shade of pink. Since he is a brown mouse with a white underbelly, Niki mixed some

31

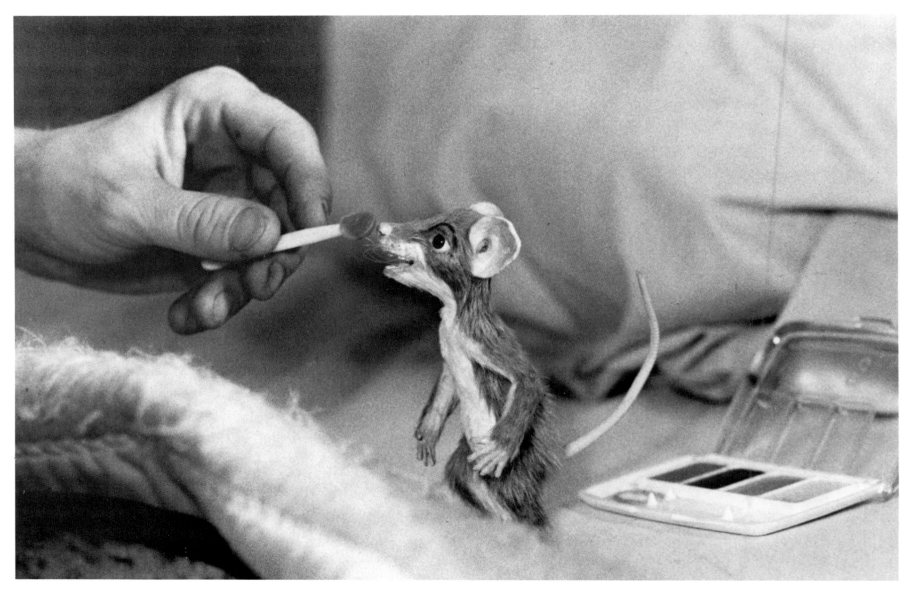

Every film star needs some makeup.

brown paint into a batch of rubber cement and brushed it on a small area. Tiny pieces of the fur were placed on this area, overlapping each other slightly, like shingles on a rooftop. She worked slowly until all of Ralph's body that needed fur was covered with it. Ralph's whiskers came from a few bristles plucked from an artist's brush. After they were glued in place, she curled them with her curling iron. With all of this careful work, it isn't surprising that John said firmly, "Without Niki, I can't do the shows."

Niki chose eyeballs from a box labeled RALPH'S EYE BLINKS. Some of the eyes in this box were fully open, some were half-open, others were barely open, and others were closed. John switched the eyes during the filming, and Ralph appears to be looking around at his world with surprise, fear, humor, weariness, and all the other expressions that eyes can reflect.

With the mice finished, the three months of preproduction work were completed. The actors who play the parts of Ryan, Matt, and all the other characters in Mrs. Cleary's story were ready to begin the eleven-day production period at Churchill's studio in Los Angeles.

CHAPTER FOUR

Decisions! Decisions! Decisions!

As an animator, John Matthews brings inanimate objects to life—or makes them appear to have life. Since living things move, John's puppets run, walk, talk, sing, dance, roll their eyes, bounce on beds, swing across the room on venetian-blind cords—in short, they are animated in ways that are limited only by John's imagination.

John and Niki have created six Ralph puppets. Four worked in the film, and two were extras, in case something happened to one of the four. John controlled two of the mice by cables. One mouse had long cables leading to a control box that was kept at a distance. The other was John's mouse-on-a-stick. The cables for this version of Ralph ran through a short piece of metal tubing and were attached to a trigger control at its base. John used the mouse-on-a-stick when actors had to handle Ralph.

Perhaps the simplest form of animation is something called a wire gag. A wire so thin it is almost invisible is attached to a *dead mouse* (John's term for a puppet with no armature) and the puppet is pulled along in front of the camera. John and his animators do not use wire gags often, and when they do, it is only for a brief period of time. Most of the animation John does is created through stop-motion photography. This is an animation process that uses thousands of photographs—each with the subject in a slightly different position—to achieve the illusion of life.

John had to decide what kind of animation he would use each time he moved Ralph, and he used a storyboard to help him make those decisions. All television shows and movies have storyboards. They help the producer and director plan how the show will be photographed. Normally, a storyboard is simply a leather binder with small clear plastic pockets. Information about each scene is written on pieces of paper and slipped into these pockets in the order in which the scenes will be filmed. An animated show has a storyboard with information about each scene, too, but it is illustrated.

Stuart Ellis illustrated the storyboard for *Ralph S. Mouse*. In order to do this, Stuart attended meetings in which the directors and producers discussed every scene in the film. He then drew a sketch of what the camera would see with each shot it took. For example, on day four of the filming, the action took place on the school bus as Ryan and Ralph, who is tucked into Ryan's back-pack, travel to the Irwin J. Sneed Elementary School. Stuart sketched the interior of the bus with Ryan and Ralph. Next to his sketch, Stuart noted the position of the camera, such as "Camera pushes in"—meaning the camera would be rolled in for a close-up. Stuart also noted any dialogue that was to be said, such as:

RALPH: "Got anything to eat in your pockets? I'm starving."
RYAN: "I think there're some cookies in my lunch."

The storyboard also includes information about actions in a shot. In this shot, Stuart wrote, "Ryan clears the frost from the window and peers out."

Tom Smith, who was the executive producer for the film *Honey, I Shrunk the Kids*, directed the actors in the live-action part of the film. He and John Matthews, director of the animated sequences, studied the storyboard, planning how the live action and animation would work together. John circled the sketch of Ryan listening to Ralph ask for something to eat, and wrote *cable* underneath it. That way, he knew to use a cable-controlled Ralph for that scene.

As he worked through the storyboard, John was able to notice anything in the script that might need to be changed to accommodate his animation. For example, in Beverly Cleary's book and again in the script, Miss Kuckenbacker asks to hold Ralph when Ryan takes him to school for the first time. John wanted the line changed to read, "Can I touch him?"

Stuart Ellis sketched the storyboard that John Matthews used to plan his animation.

Ralph-on-a-stick comes to life for John Matthews, Joel Fletcher, and Tom Smith.

"If Karen Black is just touching Ralph, I can use the mouse-on-a-stick for animation. If she holds him, she'll have to keep her hands in one position for nearly four hours while I do stop-motion animation. Nobody can keep their hands that still for that long—at least, not easily," he explained. Tom and Stuart agreed that the line should be changed, and it was. When a book is adapted for television or the movies, changes frequently have to be made because it is simply too difficult, or too expensive, to follow the author's original dialogue exactly. With the help of the storyboard and a few changes in the dialogue, John was able to plan exactly which kind of Ralph puppet would be needed for each day of shooting.

Although the production period lasted only eleven days, they were busy, tense ones. Churchill's Los Angeles studio was crowded. In addition to the cast, there was a large crew working together to make this television show come to life. The crew included the producers, directors, animators, and model makers about whom you have read, as well as Howard Wexler, the director of photography, assistants for him and director Tom Smith, people to work the sound systems, electricians, script supervisors, caterers to serve everyone lunch, a teacher for the child actors, people to do wardrobe and makeup, and a fire marshal. In all, fifty-eight people were employed during the production part of this film.

The first day of production on any television show or movie is a bit like the first day of school. Everyone is excited, and just a bit nervous. Ralph was there to break the tension, though. Everyone smiled as John unpacked one of the puppets and carefully placed him on his motorcycle. Joel reached for Ralph's Ping-Pong ball safety helmet and attempted to put it on the puppet. It didn't fit! Once again, the problem was Ralph's ears, which were slightly larger than the previous puppet's, so the helmet had to be modified, just like the car's bubble top. Joel whisked out his penknife and carved away just enough space to accommodate Ralph's new, improved movable ears.

John picked up his Ralph-on-a-stick and practiced moving the puppet's head around, talking in his "Ralph" voice to Karen Black. She looked at the mouse, smiled, then

A film set is a crowded and busy place.

"Can I touch him?" Karen Black asks in rehearsal.

John was on the set every day, because he and Tom had to plan the ways they were going to photograph Ralph with the rest of the cast. When Ralph appeared "live" with the actors, John had to animate him by cable. Depending on the camera angle, John could be comfortable while he did this work, or he could be very uncomfortable indeed. For example, during the scene in which Miss Kuckenbacker asks to touch Ralph, John was able to squat behind the teacher's lectern and animate Ralph easily. And furthermore, he could see what Ralph and Miss Kuckenbacker looked like as they acted together.

There were times, however, when John was forced to

John Matthews watches the action with the help of a monitor.

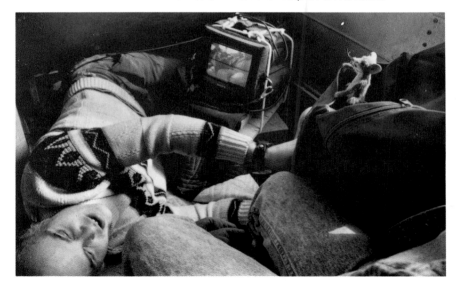

looked at John. "I read the book. He's very real to me," she said.

John made Ralph answer, indignantly, "Of course I'm real!"

Karen laughed. She was caught up in Ralph's magic. "You do lie a bit, you know," she said to the mouse.

"I do *not*," John answered for Ralph. "Sometimes I just avoid the truth."

John and Karen were still smiling at this exchange when Tom Smith called for everyone on the set. He was eager to begin production, and so was the rest of the cast and crew. There was much work to do.

operate Ralph without being able to see what the mouse or the actor was doing. The scene with Ralph and Ryan on the school bus is a good example. During preproduction, John cut a hole in the bus seat and a matching hole in the bottom of Ryan's backpack. Ralph-on-a-stick was inserted through both of these holes while John lay on the floor of the crowded school bus. He was out of the camera's way, but he couldn't see what he was doing with Ralph. In order to solve that problem, John placed a special picture monitor in easy view. Cables attached the monitor to a television camera, so by looking at the monitor, John was able to see exactly what director Tom Smith and photography director Howard Wexler were seeing.

John does not like to use cable animation very much, because it is so limiting to the puppet. He reserved it for the times Ralph was rooted to one spot, such as when he peeked from the top of Ryan's backpack or his shirt pocket. John said, "I much prefer doing the kind of animation where Ralph zooms around on his motorcycle or tumbles into a wastebasket." John used stop-motion photography to achieve those effects; however, that process did not begin until the production period was over.

Although cable isn't John's favorite kind of animation, most actors prefer it. It is always easier to say lines to a real person, or mouse, than it is to say them to a blank space. During the cable animation, Ralph was there for the actors to speak to, working his special kind of magic.

John uses a cable to control Ralph when he is in Ryan's pocket.

However, the actors had to be prepared to speak to Ralph, even if the puppet wasn't there. They said their lines to a blank space where Ralph would be—later. If the camera angle was just right and it wasn't going to be photographed, John or Tom could put a dummy mouse in the spot where Ralph would be—just to help the actors focus their eyes properly. Then the scene was filmed—a process called shooting plates. The film, or plate, of the scene formed a background for John to use when he animated Ralph in a few specific scenes later in the postproduction period.

41

CHAPTER FIVE

Mice on the Move

During the eleven-day production period of *Ralph S. Mouse,* at least thirty people were on the set every day, and excitement and tension filled the air. Speaking about this period, John said, "It isn't my favorite time to work. I like the peace and quiet of postproduction better." During postproduction, when most of the animation was completed, only John and his animators were in the studio. The atmosphere was quiet and relaxed, and John and his crew were finally alone with their puppets.

However, before any animation could begin, things had to be set up. During production, the human actors shot some background plates—in other words, they filmed scenes as if Ralph was in them, though he was not. During postproduction, everything on the set—the props, the furniture, and the lighting—had to be identical to the way it was when the background plate was shot; nothing could be out of place, not even a shadow. During production, lighting a set for one scene can take an hour or more, but matching that lighting during postproduction can take even longer.

Finally, when everything on the set was perfect, the animation could begin. As exciting as an animated film is to watch, John explained that watching the animator work at his craft is not exciting. "It's a bit like watching paint dry or ice cubes melt," he said with a smile.

John used a special camera for his stop-motion animation work. This type of camera is different from the one used to film the live action. The film ran through that camera at a steady rate and stopped only when the director yelled "Cut!" The animation camera is a type of movie camera that is capable of taking pictures one frame at a time. Inside the camera a single frame is held behind the lens. When the animator pushes a button, the shutter opens and one image is photographed. John had to reposition and rephotograph Ralph twenty-four times for each second of film.

John and Tom Smith worked together to decide on each scene's camera angle. The camera's placement determines how the audience will view each scene. If they see it from Ralph's point of view, the camera will become Ralph. In other words, it had to be set close to the floor—at mouse height. On the other hand, if the audience is watching from Ryan's point of view, then the camera had to be set at human height. At other times, the camera was positioned as if it were a member of the audience and then it

The Laser XL7—from Ralph's point of view

photographed the scenes from a more distant, or pulled-back, perspective. During postproduction animation shooting, most of the scenes were shot at mouse height.

Since there was more than one Ralph puppet, he could be in two places at once, which makes animated filming far more efficient than production filming. Live actors cannot be in more than one place at a time! John had a team of animators to help him, so Ralph could be on the set of Ryan's bedroom, tumbling from a windowsill at the same time he is in Miss Kuckenbacker's classroom, swinging on the end of the blind cord. John discussed each scene with his animators, telling them what he wanted Ralph to do. However, he allowed his animators to decide just how they would get Ralph to do it.

For those scenes in which Ralph is suspended in midair, the animators used a flying rig to help them. A flexible and thin wire called a monofilament was attached to a clamp that was fastened to the end of an adjustable stand. The wire had to be strong enough to support the puppet, but so thin that the camera would not photograph it easily. If the wire broke in the middle of a shot, all the careful work of animating would have to be repeated, so the animators experimented with different gauges, or thicknesses, of monofilament until they found just the right one. Since the wire might have reflected light, it was darkened with a black felt pen. Joel Fletcher used a flying rig and monofilament as he animated the scene of Ralph flying across the classroom. In describing the wire, Joel said, "By the time I was finished with that wire, even *I* had a hard time seeing it!"

Animation involves much more than just moving puppets from here to there. A good animator thinks not only about how his puppet will move but also about what its face or its body will be expressing as it moves. When Ralph paces on the windowsill of Ryan's bedroom, he is talking to himself, worrying about whether he should stay at the Mountain View Inn or leave. If he stays, Matt will lose his job. On the other hand, if he leaves, he could be eaten by an owl or freeze in the snow. As he thought about Ralph's situation and animating it, John decided to make Ralph pace back and forth on the windowsill on two feet— or paws—rather than on four. "It's a little harder to animate him on two feet," John said, "but I wanted him to

Ralph flies through the air—with the help of monofilament wire.

stand up and sink down as he argued with himself. I think the pacing, along with the rising and sinking, help the viewers understand Ralph's dilemma. He's got a really tough decision to make."

Even though walking on two feet is a decidedly unmouselike movement, because John had studied the motions of living mice, he understood how a mouse _would_ walk on two feet if he just could. Explaining further, he said, "Animators must study how things move. If you're going to animate mice, you've got to know how a real mouse moves before you can take liberties with that movement in your puppet."

Ralph paces on two feet as he thinks about his problems.

In any cable-controlled animation, the puppet's movements are limited by its cables in much the same way as a marionette is controlled by its strings. And just as a marionette moves on a stage, the puppet moves in front of the camera, so—unlike stop-motion photography—cable-controlled animation becomes a film of real movement.

Stop-motion animation is actually a series of still photographs that, when projected onto a screen, appear to move. When John animated using this process, Ralph's movements were limited only by John's imagination. If John thought of it, Ralph would be able to do it. In order to do stop-motion animation, a projector is needed to project the film frame by frame. Inside the projector, the film is pulled past a powerful beam of light. When a frame is in front of the light, the shutter opens and one image of Ralph is projected onto the screen—for one twenty-fourth of a second. The shutter then closes until the next frame is ready, then it opens and another image appears for another twenty-fourth of a second. For each animated minute of _Ralph S. Mouse_ that you see, 1,440 different images will flash in front of your eyes.

When the human eye sees something, the brain retains the image of it for a split second after it disappears. This phenomenon is called persistence of vision. While the screen is dark, the brain "remembers" the previous frame of Ralph, and by the time that "memory" is fading, a new image is on the screen. During the animated portions of _Ralph S. Mouse_ or any other animated or live-action film,

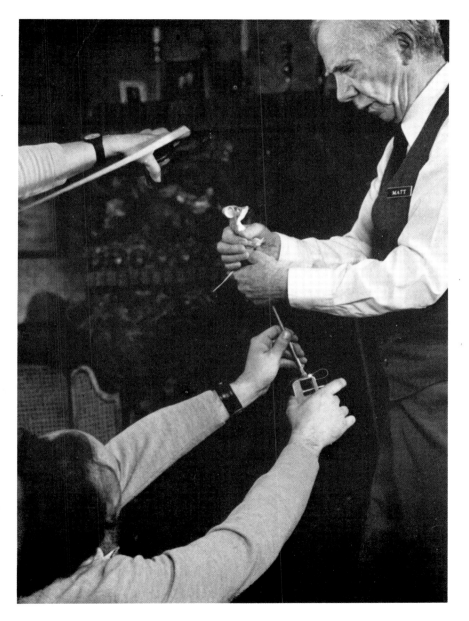

The mouse-on-a-stick has a chat with Matt.

the screen is actually dark longer than it is filled with an image. However, due to humans' persistence of vision, no one sees the darkness. Nevertheless, the darkness is necessary. If it was not there, the images would all run together and become a blur.

The juggling Ralph on the corner of the pages of this book is an example of stop-motion animation. Flip the corners of the pages, and Ralph appears to move. There are not many pages in this book, so there were not many opportunities to change Ralph's positions. Therefore, this animation is not at all as elaborate as the animation you see on television or in feature-length films, which can have as many as 1 million separate frames, or pictures, with a split second of darkness separating each one.

The art of animation does not lie in cameras or projectors, however. Instead, it requires vision and judgment on the part of the animator. It is the animator who decides exactly what moves the puppet makes so that the action flows freely. You have seen crudely animated characters who move in a jerky, unnatural fashion. "Getting it to look real is the hard thing," John said, then added, "The puppets can't move too much or too little, or they'll look stiff and unnatural." Ralph moved twenty-four times for each second of film that was shot. While they were working, each of John's animators had to remember that twenty-four-to-one ratio, and judge the puppet's movements accordingly. The animators had to ease Ralph into

47

Ralph's line: "Say, you gonna eat all those peanut-butter cookies by yourself?"

each new position and then ease him out of it in a series of movements that were smooth. "Many animators do things too slowly," John said. "For example, it should take Ralph only a half second to tumble from the windowsill and bounce onto Ryan's bed—six frames for the tumble itself, and six frames for the bounce when he lands. When Ralph hits the bed, he will go down, down, down, up, up, then down."

As you can see, a lot of careful thought and planning goes into each second of animation that is shown. Animators have to keep track of each of their puppet's movements. In order to do this, all of John's animators use a device called a surface gauge. The surface gauge shows exactly where something was, which makes it easier for an animator to judge where it should be in the next frame. For example, at the beginning of each scene, Ralph was placed where he had to be, and his body was positioned the way John wanted it. Everything was adjusted—his eyes, his ears, his tail, even his mouth. Once everything was properly placed, surface gauges were brought out to measure the precise position of all these parts of Ralph. The gauges were adjusted to the proper position, then carefully removed. John sighted through his animation camera, and if he was satisfied with what he saw, he took a picture that will be seen for one twenty-fourth of a second. Next, the gauge was returned to its original position over the puppet. Without disturbing the gauge, the puppet was moved slightly in relation to the gauge. In this new position, everything was readjusted

A surface gauge helps the animator keep track of Ralph's position.

again—eyes, mouth, ears, body, tail—nothing was overlooked, even though the movement was so slight, only an animator would have noticed it. John or an animator studied Ralph in his new position as it compared to the surface gauge, which allowed them to "see" Ralph in his old position. Once all adjustments were made, the surface gauge was removed, and once again John took a single picture, which was scarcely different from the previous one, but different nonetheless. This picture, too, appears on the screen for one twenty-fourth of a second. Again, the surface gauge was replaced, the puppet was removed and repositioned, and the process repeated itself—twenty-four separate pictures for each second of movement on the screen. In all, it took 28,800 separate frames or pictures to animate the two twenty-two minute segments that compose the *Ralph S. Mouse* film.

You have seen how Ralph was animated when he was working alone on the deserted movie set during post-production. You also have seen how John used cables to control Ralph when he was appearing with the actors on those same sets during production. But what of those scenes—the background plates—that the actors shot during production, acting as if Ralph was there when he was not? In the final stages of animation, John had to put Ralph back into those scenes. He did this by using a technique called process projection, in which he used the background plates that were shot during production and more stop-motion photography for animation.

Some of the most exciting advances in the art of animation have come in recent years when live action and animation were combined in a story. Audiences thrilled to see actors talking to celluloid characters in *Who Framed Roger Rabbit?*, or to puppets in *E. T.*, or any of the three shows about Ralph S. Mouse. Only the most skillful animators can bring human actors and puppets or celluloid drawings together in a way that makes the audience believe something like that really could happen. Process projection makes those scenes believable.

John began by placing a puppet stage in front of a screen. Then the background plate was loaded into the projector and a single frame was projected onto the screen. When the background image—perhaps Ryan

Ryan rescues Ralph from Mr. Costa's mousetrap.

speaking sleepily to Ralph after the mouse has bounced onto his bed—filled the screen, John placed his puppet on the stage. He positioned Ralph as if he were responding to the projected image behind him, and lighted the stage to match the lighting in the background plate. Then the animation proceeded as before, frame by frame, twenty-four frames per second, with John coordinating and photographing the movements of the puppet as Ralph reacted to the scene on the screen behind him. John and his animation team are so skillful that one cannot tell which scenes were animated by cable, which were animated on the set, and which used background plates to achieve the illusion of mouse and boy talking and playing together.

The sound for any film, whether it is shown in movie theaters or on television, is recorded on magnetic tapes called tracks. The actors' dialogue is recorded on one sound track during production, while the background music and sound effects are recorded on other sound tracks later, during postproduction. By the time the film is edited, most of the sound tracks are on it, so the editor can hear as well as see what each scene is like. "Music and sound effects really add to the reality of animation," John said. "You need a *ba-rump, ba-rump, ba-rump* sound when Ralph is running, and a *Whoa-a-a* when he tumbles off the windowsill."

John was able to add a few sound effects such as *ba-rump* and *whoa-a-a* during the editing process; however, most of the sound work, including the voices of the mice and the background music, was recorded during postproduction in a sound studio. John is the voice of Ralph. To record Ralph, John spoke in falsetto—a range that is higher than a man's natural voice. His voice was then raised even higher by an electronic device called a harmonizer. The result is a squeaky tone totally unlike John's soft voice, but very appropriate for a mouse.

Will Ryan recorded the voices of the other mice. Will has worked as an actor in front of the camera and onstage, but he is best known in the entertainment industry for voice work. Among other things, Will has provided voices for characters in *An American Tail*, *The Little Mermaid*, and *Mickey's Christmas Carol*. Will also has worked with John Matthews, doing voices for Churchill's produc-

The voices of the mice are recorded in a sound studio.

tions of Arnold Lobel's Frog and Toad stories and Syd Hoff's story *Stanley and the Dinosaurs.*

Will and John worked together to create the special music for *Ralph S. Mouse.* Together, they composed "Stretchercize," a song and exercise routine Miss Kuckenbacker uses each day to wake up her class. Other musicians were brought to the sound studio to provide background voices. John directed the recording sessions at the studio, and everyone involved had a very good time.

In addition to brilliant animation, editing, sound effects, and music all contribute to the believability and magic of the film version of *Ralph S. Mouse.*

55

·

CHAPTER SEVEN

Claymation and Cartoons

Up until this point, this discussion has centered on three-dimensional animation—the kind that is done with puppets. You have read about how Ralph was given brass bones and foam-rubber flesh. However, there is one other kind of three-dimensional animation that is easily recognized by television viewers. These puppets have brass bones, too, but their flesh is made of clay. Claymation is the name its creator, Will Vinton, has given to this form of animation. Perhaps the best-known example of Claymation artistry is the California Raisins. Sponsored by the California Raisin Advisory Board, these carefully carved puppets strutted their way into popularity singing "I Heard It Through the Grapevine." The California Raisin commercials have won three Clio awards, which are the advertising industry's equivalent of an Oscar or an Emmy.

Claymation uses the same kinds of animation techniques that John Matthews used with Ralph. Stop-motion photography makes the puppets sing and dance. Although their clay flesh is molded to varying shapes easily, some animators have said that these kinds of puppets are difficult to work with because they are easily damaged by fingerprints and excessive handling. Nevertheless, no matter how difficult this animation may be to achieve, it is clear that the public loves watching it. Raisin sales in the United States soared 20 percent after those famous commercials caught on.

No discussion of animation would be complete without mentioning celluloid animation, or, as it is commonly known, cartoons. For decades, cartoons were the only kind of animation seen in movie theaters or on television. Fifty years ago, audiences laughed at the antics of characters such as Walt Disney's Mickey Mouse or Hanna-Barbera's Tom and Jerry. Mickey, Tom and Jerry, and many others are still popular today. However, they share their popularity with more modern cartoon characters, such as the Simpsons. According to their creator, cartoonist Matt Groening, the Simpsons are a middle-of-the-road American family who can be much wilder than live-action families, simply because they are animated.

It is true that drawn cartoon characters are two-dimensional and therefore far less realistic than their three-dimensional puppet counterparts. However, it is this very absence of realism that allows cartoon characters to do completely fantastic feats such as jumping over

Walt Disney's Mickey Mouse debuted as Steamboat Willie. (*Steamboat Willie* © The Walt Disney Company.)

a skyscraper in a single bound, or falling off a cliff and bouncing back up again with no harm done. Although it would be easy to achieve, this kind of rather violent animation is not done with three-dimensional puppets because it would be unbelievable and inappropriate.

Although he prefers working with puppets, John Mat-

John Matthews created the cartoon shown in *Runaway Ralph.*

thews has done cartoon animation. He understands that everyone loves the cartoons—including Ralph and his cousins. At the very beginning of *Runaway Ralph,* there is a scene of Ralph and his cousins watching a cartoon on television in the lobby of the Mountain View Inn. John created the small piece of cartoon the mice are watching.

Although John's cartoon is not complete, the methods he used are identical to the methods used to create full-length feature cartoons, such as *The Little Mermaid.*

Like all animators, cartoonists depend on storyboards to help them organize the film. A layout artist looks at the storyboard and makes decisions about each scene, such as what the background will be and how the characters will behave and move. Next, background artists draw everything that will appear in each scene, except the characters themselves. They are drawn by the animators.

Just as John Matthews and his team studies the movements of mice to prepare them for the Ralph series, the animators who worked on *The Little Mermaid* studied actress Sherri Stoner to help them understand some things about Ariel, their little mermaid. In one instance, Sherri had to submerge herself in a tank of water every day for three days while the animators studied how her long hair moved underwater!

As in all animation, a cartoon character's movements must be smooth. The characters must ease into and out of their movements, just as the puppets do. In order to achieve this smoothness, the animators create one drawing, or cel, for each frame of film. The character is in a slightly different position in each new cel. The animator pays attention to body movements, as well as facial expressions and mouth movements. Cel animators use a timing chart to help them know how many separate cels will have to be drawn to express each word of the dialogue. A simple two-syllable word such as *hello* could require eight separate drawings.

Once the drawings are complete, they are traced onto transparent pieces of celluloid. The characters are drawn on top of the celluloid, and a separate team of artists paints them in on the reverse side. When all of the draw-

The animators used a live model to help them draw the cartoon character, the Little Mermaid. (*The Little Mermaid* © The Walt Disney Company.)

ings, or cels, are ready, the animation process can begin. Each cel is laid over the appropriate background scene, then photographed with a single-frame animation camera. When the film is projected at the proper speed, the cartoon characters come to life and scamper across the screen just as Ralph does.

When moving pictures were born and Thomas Edison invented his boxlike kinetoscope, he realized that an important element was missing—an audience. He wanted to share his creation with more than one person at a time, and so, as you have read, he went on to invent the technique of projection so that entire groups of people could watch his films. Movie producers today feel exactly as Edison did so long ago. No matter how wonderful, exciting, and inventive their films are, they are nothing without an audience. Movie and television critics may write reviews about new television shows, but the reaction of the viewing audience is the most important review of all. By tuning it in or turning it off, the television audience decides whether a show will remain on the air, be shown in reruns, or die an early death.

George McQuilkin and John Matthews were anxious to get an audience's opinion about their new project before it was shown on ABC. Accordingly, they decided to premier *Ralph S. Mouse* at the Gallery Theatre in Hollywood, California. The event was called A Festival of Films from Around the World. It was sponsored by the Junior Arts Center and the Children's Film and Television Center of America. Children's films from many different countries were shown during this event, and *Ralph S. Mouse* was the first that was seen. It was shown twice on its premier day—first to an audience of about four hundred boys and girls from different neighborhoods throughout Los An-

geles, and a few hours later to an audience of film critics, producers, and other interested adults. Of the two audiences, George and John cared most about the children's reaction. After all, the film was really made for them.

Once the young audience had seen the show, the children were asked to evaluate it on specially prepared forms. Ninety-nine percent said the show was "excellent."

Everyone waited anxiously for an invitation to the premiere.

Churchill Entertainment
invites you and a guest to attend a special screening of

Ralph S. Mouse

An ABC Weekend Special
Based on the novel by Beverly Cleary

Saturday, January 19, 1991 • 4:00 p.m.

The Gallery Theatre
Barnsdall Art Park • 4814 Hollywood Boulevard
Children Welcome

A reception honoring the cast and crew will follow
on the Junior Arts Center patio adjacent to the Gallery

R.S.V.P. (seating limited)

The remaining 1 percent graded it "very good." One child wrote on his evaluation form, "I loved this show. I've never read that book, but now I will." That young person will join the ranks of those millions of readers who have made Ralph a major literary character. Now, thanks to the art of animation, and the reaction of audiences around the world, Ralph has become a television star, as well.

The filming is over and Ralph's work is done.

Afterword

Everyone has heard of the Oscars and the Emmys, awards that honor excellence in movies and television, respectively. The Association for Library Service to Children, which is a division of the American Library Association, gives awards for excellence, too. Each year, the Newbery Medal is awarded to the book, published the previous year, that is considered to be the most distinguished contribution to children's literature for that year. Similarly, each year the Caldecott Medal goes to the best-illustrated picture book. In 1991, the American Library Association established a new award, called the Andrew Carnegie Medal. It joins the ranks of the Newbery and Caldecott medals, since it, too, stands for excellence. It honors the most outstanding children's video released in the previous year. On January 14, 1991, the first Andrew Carnegie Medal for Excellence in Children's Video was awarded to George McQuilkin and John Matthews for *Ralph S. Mouse*.

Ralph S. Mouse

A Churchill Entertainment Production of an
ABC Weekend Special

Based on the Novel by
Beverly Cleary

Produced by
John Clark Matthews and
George McQuilkin

Directed by
Thomas G. Smith

Director of Animation
and the Voice of Ralph
John Clark Matthews

Cast

Ryan	Robert Oliveri
Matt	Ray Walston
Miss Kuckenbacker	Karen Black
Brad	Jacob Kenner
Melissa	Sharon Batts
Mr. Costa	Britt Leach
Mr. Minch	Lou Cuttell
Emma	Kimmy Robertson
William	Austin Kelly
Gordon	J. J. Anderson II
Inez	Mary Grady
Mrs. Bramble	Susie Duff
Cameraman Rod	Jimi Bridges, Jr.
Ralph's voice	John Clark Matthews
Additional mice voices	June Foray
	Robin Levy
	Will Ryan

Crew

Co-producer	Richard David
Teleplay	Joe S. Landon
Director of Photography	Howard Wexler
Music	Steven Kohn
Animations	Joel Fletcher
	Justin Kohn
	Michael Belzer
	Gail Van Der Merwe
	Mark Kendrick
Creature Construction	Niki Matthews
Radio songs	Will Ryan
Production Designer	John Clark Matthews
Editor	Jill Nimero
Production Manager	Nomi Roth Elbert
First Assistant Director	Terry Edwards
Second Assistant Director	John Keefer
Casting	Barbara Remsen, C.S.A.
	Ann Remsen Manners
Sound Editor	Carmen Flores
Assistant Editor	Tobin Hemingway
Postproduction Assistant	Jim Belcher
Gaffer	Curtiss Bradford
Mixer	Alan Barker
Boom Operator	Hunter Crowley
Key Grip	Tim Collins
Script Supervisor	Laura Shrewsbury
Wardrobe Supervisor	Kristine Brown
Makeup/Hair	Barrie Buckner
Art Directors	David D. Johnson
	Peter Michels
	Steve Brien
Set Dresser/Property Master	Jonathan Southard
Assistant Props	

Model Maker/Assistant Props	Ray Greer
Casting Assistant	Jeanne Ashby
Extra Casting	Judy Belshe
Production Coordinator	Debbie Diaz
Production Secretary	David Lawrence
Assistant to the Producers	Fred Schaefer
Assistant Cameraperson	Aggi Lukaszewski
Best Boy Electric	Brian Robertshaw
Grip	Butch Von Bulow
Swingman	Tom Conway
Studio Teacher	Dr. Caren M. Elin
Production Assistants	Jay Lee
	Ellen Frankenstein
	Harrison Gibbs
Special Props	Wayne Tsuaki
	Brian Prosser
	Nathan Matthews
	Nigel Matthews
Rerecording	Mark Rozett
	David Yamamoto
Studio Recording	Bruce Honda
Sculpture	Stuart Land
	Dale Gordon
	Floarea Liceica
Mouse Sculpture	Joel Fletcher
	John Clark Matthews
Armatures	Justin Kohn
	Peter Marinello
	Doug Beswick
Negative Cutter	Don Sykes
Special Mouse Talent	Rick Polizzi
Effects Animation Consultant	Jim Aupperle
Animation Assistant	Peter Marinello
Storyboard Artist	Stuart Ellis

Index